Taylor
v.
Pinnacle Packaging Products, Inc.

Third Edition

Deposition Materials

Plaintiff

Taylor
v.
Pinnacle Packaging Products, Inc.

Third Edition

Deposition Materials

Plaintiff

Hon. Andrew P. Rodovich

Thomas J. Leach

University of the Pacific
McGeorge School of Law

Address inquiries to:

Reprint Permission
National Institute for Trial Advocacy
1685 38th Street, Suite 200
Boulder, CO 80301-2735
Phone: (800) 225-6482
Fax: (720) 890-7069
Email: permissions@nita.org

ISBN 978-1-60156-446-7 (print)
eISBN 978-1-63282-213-0 (eBook)
FBA 1446

Printed in the United States of America

Teaching Note

The "surprise" documents that Taylor, Roberts, and Hamilton bring to their preparation sessions (Exhibits T-1, R-1, H-1, and H-2) can be used fruitfully in a longer, more advanced course. They bring to light lively issues of witness preparation and the ethics of "sandpapering" the witness. They test the preparing lawyers' ability to elicit the fullest, most truthful account from the witnesses, just as they test the deposing lawyers' ability to cope with a newly discovered document and the issues it raises.

We suggest that these additional documents be omitted from a basic, or shorter, course.

Contents

INTRODUCTION

On May 11, YR-2, the plaintiff, Jamie Taylor, was hired by the defendant, Pinnacle Packaging Products Inc., to work in the warehouse. Pursuant to company policy, the plaintiff was considered a probationary employee for sixty days. The plaintiff was fired by the warehouse manager, John Hamilton, on June 22, YR-2. The plaintiff alleges that she was fired because she resisted Hamilton's advances.

The applicable law is contained in the final instructions at the end of the case file.

The plaintiff's witnesses at trial (all of whom may be deposed by the defendant in this deposition course) will include:

Jamie Taylor

Lisa Roberts

Jerry Black

The defendant's witnesses at trial (all of whom may be deposed by the plaintiff in this deposition course) will include:

John Hamilton

Chuck Singleton

Michelle Johnson

UNITED STATES DISTRICT COURT
NORTHERN DISTRICT OF NITA
DARROW DIVISION

Jamie TAYLOR, Plaintiff	:	
	:	
v.	:	CAUSE NO. YR-1 cv 321
	:	
PINNACLE PACKAGING PRODUCTS INC., Defendant	:	JURY DEMAND

COMPLAINT

Comes now the Plaintiff, Jamie Taylor, and for cause of action against the Defendant, Pinnacle Packaging Products Inc., alleges:

1. On May 11, YR-2, the Plaintiff was hired to work on the packaging line in the warehouse of the Defendant.
2. During her employment, the Plaintiff was sexually harassed by the warehouse manager, John Hamilton, who repeatedly asked the Plaintiff to go out with him.
3. When the Plaintiff refused the sexual advances of Hamilton, she was terminated without cause on June 22, YR-2.
4. The Plaintiff timely filed a charge with the Equal Employment Opportunity Commission and received a right to sue letter within the last ninety days.

WHEREFORE the Plaintiff, Jamie Taylor, DEMANDS judgment against the Defendant, Pinnacle Packaging Products Inc., for compensatory damages and all other appropriate relief.

Filed: 2/11/YR-1

Maurice Howard

Attorney for Plaintiff

UNITED STATES DISTRICT COURT

NORTHERN DISTRICT OF NITA

DARROW DIVISION

Jamie TAYLOR, Plaintiff	: : :	
v.	: :	CAUSE NO. YR-1 cv 321
PINNACLE PACKAGING PRODUCTS INC., Defendant	: : :	JURY DEMAND

ANSWER TO COMPLAINT

Comes now the Defendant, Pinnacle Packaging Products Inc., and in answer to the Plaintiff's complaint states:

1. Admit.
2. Deny.
3. Defendant admits that the Plaintiff was terminated on June 22, YR-2, but denies the remaining allegations of paragraph 3.
4. Admit.

Wherefore, the Defendant, Pinnacle Packaging Products Inc., demands judgment against the Plaintiff, Jamie Taylor, and for all other appropriate relief.

AFFIRMATIVE DEFENSE

Comes now the Defendant, Pinnacle Packaging Products Inc., and for an affirmative defense states that it had a company policy against all forms of sex discrimination and that the Plaintiff unreasonably failed to follow that policy and report any instances of sexual harassment.

Filed: 3/5/YR-1

Attorney for Defendant

Plaintiff's Confidential Materials

Statement of Jamie Taylor

My name is Jamie Taylor, and my date of birth is March 21, YR-23. I have a high school diploma, and I have had several jobs since high school. In May YR-2, my friend, Lisa Roberts, told me that her company, Pinnacle Packaging Products, was looking for some people to work on the packaging line in the warehouse. Lisa and I have been friends since high school, and she got me a job application from the warehouse manager, John Hamilton. I submitted my application and was hired after an interview with Hamilton.

My first day of work was May 11, YR-2. I was scheduled to work the 8:00 a.m. to 4:30 p.m. shift. All new employees have a probationary status for sixty days. I was paid $9.50 per hour and was scheduled to work a forty-hour week. After my probationary status was completed, I would have received medical insurance and other benefits. I started working on a packaging line, and my immediate foreman was Chuck Singleton. I started work on Monday, and the first week went without incident.

Because Friday was Singleton's birthday, several employees on our lines decided to take him out for drinks after work. We went to Kool's Korner, about one mile from the company. I had ridden to work with Lisa all week, so she drove me to Kool's Korner. About twenty people showed up after work, and we all were standing around because there were not enough seats for everyone. Some people stayed for one or two drinks, and only seven or eight of us were left by 7:00 p.m. Lisa and I pushed two tables together and sat down.

Hamilton had arrived at Kool's Korner about one hour after everyone else, and I had not talked to him that evening. I was a little surprised when he sat down next to me. Of course, Singleton was still there, and he sat across the table from Hamilton.

We all talked for another hour, and Hamilton bought a round of drinks for the table. By this time, I believe that I had four drinks. I felt a little light-headed because I was drinking on an empty stomach. Lisa was having a good time, and her boyfriend, Mark Stewart, had joined the party and was sitting next to Lisa. It did not appear as though she would be leaving anytime soon.

The dress code of Pinnacle is casual, and I was wearing a pair of jeans and a sweatshirt. Because Lisa was talking to Mark, I spent most of my time talking to Hamilton and Singleton. Without warning, Hamilton put his hand on my knee. I did not know what to do, so I did not say anything. I tried to act like nothing was happening and continued our conversation. Apparently, Hamilton was encouraged because I had not done anything, so he moved his hand a little further up my thigh. I moved closer to Lisa and turned my leg, and his hand came off my leg.

I was anxious to leave the bar and asked Lisa when she was going home. She had just ordered another drink, and Lisa said she would leave when she finished it. Hamilton told me that he was planning on leaving and asked me whether I wanted a ride home. I was reluctant to leave with him, but I did not want to wait around for Lisa. I told Hamilton that I would accept the ride from him.

I live at 1234 Main Street, which is about three miles from Kool's Korner. There are eight apartments in my building, and my apartment overlooks Main Street. Hamilton did not say anything on the ride home that concerned me. When we stopped in front of my apartment building, he started to tell me that I was doing a good job at work. He also said that I would get a raise when I completed my probationary period. He told me that Singleton made recommendations on who was promoted but that he had the final say.

As he was talking to me, he put his hand on my knee again. I was concerned because we were alone and the street was not well lit. I did not pull away, but I told him that I had to leave because I had to get up early on Saturday. Hamilton then leaned over and kissed me good night. I was so surprised that I did not resist or try to push him away. I quickly said good night and got out of his car. When I got inside, I called Lisa on her cell phone to tell her what had happened. She still was at the bar, and I could tell that she was having a good time. She laughed it off and commented that he was not the worst guy I had been out with. I told Lisa that I would see her Monday morning.

On May 18, YR-2, I returned to work for the 8:00 a.m. shift. I saw Hamilton in his office talking to Singleton. Hamilton's office is near the employee entrance to the warehouse. The front wall of his office is mostly glass. The lower three feet is made of concrete blocks, and everything else is windows. I tried not to look into the office and walked directly to my work site.

Hamilton normally walks through the warehouse several times during the shift. Sometimes he stops and talks to a worker or Singleton, and other times he watches what is going on before returning to his office. Around 9:30 a.m., Hamilton walked up to me and asked whether I had a good weekend. He did not talk long, and neither one of us said anything about Friday evening. Later that day, Singleton moved my work station over to in front of the window into Hamilton's office, which I thought was strange—what were they watching me so closely for? Exhibit 11 is an accurate diagram of the warehouse, and I have marked it to show my two different work stations.

I did not have any problems with Singleton during my first week on the job. On Monday, Singleton criticized me for not working fast enough and for taking too many bathroom breaks. Hamilton did not say anything to me about my job performance on Monday, and he only stopped to talk to me that one time in the morning.

The criticism that started on Monday continued during the rest of the week. It seemed like Singleton was watching me all the time and waiting for something to complain about. Lisa did not work on the same packaging line, but I complained to her about Singleton.

When I returned to work on Monday, May 25, YR-2, Singleton was waiting for me with a written reprimand. It stated that I spent too much time away from my work station and that I was not meeting the production quotas. He also told me that I had to meet with Hamilton before starting work.

Singleton and I waited in Hamilton's office for him to arrive. Shortly after 8:00 a.m., Hamilton came in, and Singleton gave him a copy of the reprimand. Hamilton read the write-up and reminded me that I was on probation. He also said that any additional write-ups would affect his decision on whether I would become a full-time employee.

Singleton and I started to leave the office when Hamilton told me that I had to sign the reprimand. I signed it and gave it back to him. Before I could leave the office, Hamilton told me that I was much prettier when I smiled. I told him that I did not feel like smiling, and he said that I should not worry about my job. As I turned to leave, Hamilton asked me whether I would join him for a few drinks after work. I told him that I did not think that it was a good idea.

I went directly to my work station, and I could tell Singleton was irritated by the delay in Hamilton's office. I worked as hard as I could, especially when Singleton was around.

Hamilton made his usual rounds on Monday. The first few times, he ignored me. I was convinced that he was mad at me. When he walked past me during the afternoon, I said hello and asked him how he was doing. He stopped to talk to me for a few minutes before he moved on through the warehouse.

The warehouse is not air conditioned and sometimes can get very warm. In late May, the weather was getting very warm. All of the employees dress casually, and both the men and women started wearing T-shirts. I did not think my T-shirts were too tight or suggestive.

On May 26, YR-2, Singleton complained about my outfit for the first time. It was hot in the warehouse, and I had been working hard. I rolled up the sleeves on my T-shirt and tied a knot in it just above my belly button. When he said it was inappropriate, I rolled down my sleeves and untied the knot. Jerry Black was working next to me, and he told Singleton that he was not offended by the T-shirt. Singleton made some comment that I was at work and not at the beach.

Hamilton had walked past me about fifteen minutes before Singleton, and he did not say anything about my attire. In fact, he smiled at me as he walked by.

A few days later, I wore a loose fitting T-shirt to work. On the front, it said "If you can read this, you're staring." When Black saw it, he made some comment about being a slow reader. Janet Long was working nearby. When she heard his comment, she told Black that his illiteracy finally was paying off. I laughed at her joke, but I did not say anything to either Black or Long.

Later in the morning, Hamilton walked through the warehouse. He looked at my T-shirt and made a comment about reading the fine print. Black made some comment about Hamilton having poor eyesight and needing a closer look. Hamilton laughed at the joke. I laughed at their jokes, but did not make any other comment.

A short time later, Singleton arrived and the trouble started. He told me that the T-shirt was inappropriate and that I had to turn it inside out. Black suggested that I make the change right there, but Singleton did not say anything to him. Singleton told me to reverse the T-shirt on my next break. I do not recall saying anything to Singleton about taking my T-shirt off right there.

My fourth week on the job started uneventfully. I thought that my performance was improving, and Singleton was not spending as much time in my area. However, on Thursday, June 4, YR-2, Singleton was waiting for me when I came to work. I had overslept that morning and could not ride with Lisa. I did not get to the warehouse until 8:10 a.m. That was the first time I had been late since I started at Pinnacle. Singleton told me he was writing me up for being late and my general conduct. The written reprimand mentioned that I was late, that I dressed inappropriately, and that I was a slow worker.

Singleton gave Hamilton a copy of the write-up. Hamilton told me to stop in his office on my next break when he was making his morning rounds. I went to his office just before my lunch break. Hamilton had a copy of the reprimand on his desk and started reading it. He asked me what I had to say, and I told him that I had overslept that morning. Hamilton asked me why my boyfriend had not awakened me. I told him that I did not have a boyfriend and that I was sleeping alone. He again reminded me that I was on probation and that I would not be hired as a permanent employee if I continued to have problems.

Hamilton gave me the write-up to sign before I left his office. I was leaning over the side of the desk to sign my name when he walked around behind me and bumped against me. When I turned to leave, Hamilton was standing between me and the door. He commented that if I did not have a boyfriend he would like to take me out that weekend. I said no and walked past him and out of his office.

I did not want Hamilton to be mad at me because I knew that he would make the final decision on my job. When he was walking through the warehouse that afternoon, I made a point of saying hi to him. He stopped to talk for a minute, but he did not say anything about going out or my job performance.

That Saturday afternoon, I was leaving my apartment to meet some friends and to go shopping. As I started to open the main door to the apartment building, I saw Hamilton driving down the street. I waited a minute to make sure he was gone and walked to my car. As I was pulling my car out of the parking lot, I saw Hamilton again coming from the other direction. I looked in my rearview mirror several times as I was driving down the street, but Hamilton did not turn around or attempt to follow me.

When I returned to work on Monday, June 8, YR-2, Hamilton was walking out of his office. He stopped and said hello and asked whether I had enjoyed the weekend. I told him that I had had a good weekend and asked him what he had done that weekend. He commented that he was not a "swinging single" and that his weekend had been uneventful. Neither one of us commented on him driving past my apartment on Saturday afternoon.

I was concerned about the fact that Hamilton had asked me out and had driven past my apartment. When I saw Singleton, I told him that I was being sexually harassed by Hamilton. Singleton told me it was all my fault because I was flirting with Hamilton. Singleton also asked me, "Do you want to keep your job?" and walked away.

Monday was another hot day in the warehouse. Nothing special happened that morning. After I completed my lunch break, I threw some cold water on my face and neck to cool down. My T-shirt was a little wet when I returned to my work station. Black made a comment to me about joining a wet T-shirt contest, and I asked him whether he thought that I would win. Long heard his comment and told Black that she was going to hose him down with cold water. Black made some comment about holding the hose and judging a wet T-shirt contest between Long and me. After the brief bantering, all three of us returned to work.

As luck would have it, Singleton walked past and saw my T-shirt. He again commented that my appearance was inappropriate. Black made some comment to Singleton about a company wet T-shirt contest that afternoon. Singleton just looked at Black and told him not to encourage me.

Singleton continued to watch me the rest of the week. It seemed that he came around either just before or just after a break to see whether I left early or returned late. Although Singleton sometimes would stop and talk to other employees, he never asked me how things were going or even said good morning.

On Wednesday, June 10, Lisa dropped something on her foot and had to leave the plant to have her foot x-rayed. On my afternoon break, I called a friend, Ron Harper, and asked him to pick me up after work. I left the plant shortly after 4:30 p.m. and walked to the main gate to wait for Harper. Around 5:00 p.m., Hamilton drove up to the main gate and asked me whether I needed a ride. I told him that I was waiting for a friend and did not need a ride. Hamilton asked me whether the friend was male or female, and I told him the friend was someone I worked with at my last job. I did not tell him my friend was a man because I did not think that it was any of his business. Hamilton did not repeat the question, but he continued to make small talk. I got the impression that he was waiting to see who came. A few minutes later, Harper came, and I said goodbye to Hamilton.

On Thursday morning, I drove myself to work because Lisa had a doctor's appointment. Hamilton was standing near the entrance to the warehouse when I got there. He asked me to step into his office and told me that Singleton had complained about the wet T-shirt incident. Hamilton said that Singleton did not have much of a sense of humor at work but that he was a good guy when you got to know him. Hamilton then added that I would find that he also was a great guy if I took the time to get to know him.

When I asked Hamilton whether I could go to my work station, he asked me where I had gone after work. I told him that Harper was only a friend and that he dropped me off at my apartment. Hamilton commented that if I had let him drive me home, he would have treated me to dinner. I thanked him for offering me the ride and went to my work station.

I got to my station around 8:15 a.m., and Singleton was waiting for me. Before he could say anything to me I told him that I had been talking to Hamilton. Singleton made some comment about me trying to keep my job the "old-fashioned way" and walked away. I was offended because Hamilton kept coming on to me, and I had not encouraged him. I started to tell Singleton that Hamilton was making the advances, but he waved his hands and continued to walk away.

On Monday, June 15, YR-2, Hamilton again stopped me as I entered the warehouse. He asked me whether I had a good weekend, and I said yes. He then asked me whether I had seen Harper, and I told him again that we were only friends and not dating. Hamilton also asked me whether I had spent my entire paycheck at the mall. This comment freaked me out, and I wondered how he knew that I had been shopping. I did not say anything to Hamilton about the comment, but I was concerned that he may have been stalking me.

Singleton came up to me as soon as I got to my work station. He told me that he knew that I was not late because he saw me flirting with Hamilton. I told him that I was not flirting with Hamilton and that Hamilton had stopped me on my way into the warehouse. Singleton told me that if I did a better job, I would not have to flirt with Hamilton.

I saw Michelle Johnson, the human resources director, walking through the warehouse. I left the line and walked over to tell her about my problems with Hamilton. Before I could talk to her, I looked back and saw that Singleton was staring at me. I walked past Johnson and got a drink of water before returning to the line. Singleton never took his eyes off me the entire time.

On Thursday, Hamilton stopped me as I was leaving work. He asked me to step into his office, and I did. Hamilton told me that his birthday was Saturday and asked me whether I wanted to go out and celebrate with him. I told him that I did not think it was a good idea for me to date the boss and declined his invitation. Hamilton was standing between me and the door, and I felt uncomfortable. I told him that I had to leave and walked past him.

Lisa had been off work all week because of her injured foot. On Friday, I had car problems and had to call the garage for a jump. When I arrived at work around 8:20, Singleton was waiting for me. I told him that I had car problems and that I had a receipt to prove it. Singleton told me that he was going to give me another written reprimand.

Hamilton walked through the warehouse several times on Friday and never looked at me. I felt like I was in trouble because Singleton was going to give me another write-up and Hamilton was ignoring me. As I left work on Friday, I stopped in Hamilton's office. I wished him a happy birthday and said that I hoped he had a nice weekend. He asked me whether I had changed my mind about dinner on Saturday, and I told him that I had not.

On Monday, June 22, YR-2, I rode to work with Lisa for the first time since her injury. I asked her to leave early because I did not want to be late. When I walked into the warehouse at 7:50 a.m., I did not see Singleton or Hamilton and went directly to my work station.

Long arrived a few minutes later and told me that she saw Singleton and Hamilton at the employees' entrance to the warehouse. She said that they were not really talking to each other, and it appeared as though they were looking for someone. I knew that that was not a good sign. Black came to the work area about ten minutes later. He commented on being a few minutes late and having to walk past Hamilton and Singleton. He said he just smiled and kept walking as fast as he could.

I was working around 8:15 a.m. when I saw Singleton coming in my direction. I continued to work and tried to ignore him, but he came up to me with another write-up in his hand. The first thing he said to me was "How did you sneak in?" I told him that I had punched in before 8:00 a.m. and that he could check my time card if he did not believe me. Singleton then told me that he had "another present" for me and handed me the reprimand. It stated I had been late for work on Friday and included the same complaints of being a slow worker and taking longer breaks than I was allowed. Singleton told me that Hamilton wanted to see me immediately.

I went to Hamilton's office, and he was waiting for me with a copy of the write-up. He told me that Singleton had been complaining about me from the start and that he had tried to convince Singleton to give me time to adjust to the new job. Hamilton said that it did not appear as though I had a future with the company and that I should punch out and turn in my ID badge.

I was upset because I was doing my best, and I asked Hamilton to give me some more time to work things out. I told him that I had come in early because I was late on Friday and had not wanted to be late again. Hamilton told me that I was not entitled to any more chances and that his mind was made up.

I might have some diary entries about Hamilton. I will check the diary and get you copies of any pages that have to do with Hamilton.

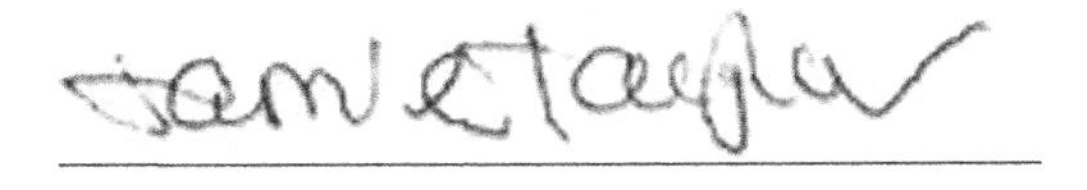

[Assume that the day before the deposition is due to be taken in this training course, Taylor came to plaintiff's counsel's office to be prepared and brought with her the document included in this file as Exhibit T-1 (available only to plaintiff), which has not heretofore been produced in discovery. Assume also that the Notice of Deposition included a standard duces tecum clause requesting the witness to bring "any and all documents relating to or concerning:

1. *Jamie Taylor's employment at Pinnacle Packaging*

2. *Hamilton's behavior toward female employees."*

You should also assume that the subpoenas that require the attendance of the other witnesses in the case file contain the same duces tecum clause.]

Exhibit T-1

Excerpts from Taylor's Diary

May 11, YR-2	Started work today at Pinnacle. Seems OK place.
May 15, YR-2	H putting the moves on me—not gonna put up with any crap.
May 25, YR-2	H & S trying to fake up reasons to fire me—BS discip report.

Statement of Lisa Roberts

My name is Lisa Roberts, and I was employed by Pinnacle Packaging Products from June YR-6 until I was terminated in May of YR-1. I worked on one of the packaging lines supervised by Chuck Singleton. John Hamilton was the warehouse manager, and Singleton reported directly to him.

I was terminated by Pinnacle after Jamie Taylor, the plaintiff in this lawsuit, filed her case against Pinnacle. In February YR-1, Jamie's lawyer asked me if I would be willing to be a witness in the case for Jamie and tell what I knew about Jamie's troubles at the company and about rumors about Hamilton's behavior to female employees. I said I would tell anything and everything I knew. I guess that news got around the plant, because in April Hamilton and Singleton called me into Hamilton's office and asked me if I was going to be a witness for Jamie. I pretended not to know anything about the lawsuit because I was afraid of what would happen to me, so I said I didn't know anything about it and I was not "planning" to be a witness. But a few weeks later, toward the end of April, Singleton started to write me up for every little thing—taking a long break, being a few minutes late in the morning, and a violation of a supposed "dress code." Then, in early May, they terminated me for "repeated lateness." I think they fired me because they were mad about me agreeing to be a witness for Jamie, which I'm sure they had a way to find out. Since then, I have been on unemployment benefits—but that's hardly enough to live on, so I have had to use all my savings just to make ends meet.

Singleton supervised the packaging lines that are adjacent to each other. If I was at my work station, I could not see what was happening on the other line. Singleton was my immediate supervisor the entire time I worked at Pinnacle.

In April YR-2, I heard that there was an opening on the other packaging line. Jamie Taylor and I have been friends since high school, and I knew that she was looking for a new job. I talked to Hamilton about Jamie, and he told me to tell Jamie to fill out a job application.

Jamie completed the application, and I brought it to work and gave it to Hamilton. A few days later, Jamie told me that she had a job interview with Hamilton. The front of Hamilton's office is mostly windows, and I could see Jamie and Hamilton talking. A short time later, I saw Hamilton showing Jamie around the warehouse.

I was returning from my lunch break when Hamilton came up to me and told me that he had hired Jamie. I thanked him for hiring her, and he said that I should tell all my other good-looking friends to apply for a job.

Jamie started working on Monday, May 11, YR-2, and I drove her to work because we were on the same shift. Jamie did not have any problems the first week, but she did say that it was hard work.

At the end of the week, we decided to go to Kool's Korner to celebrate Singleton's birthday. I drove Jamie to Kool's and called my boyfriend and told him to meet us there after work. The bar was crowded, and we all were standing around having a drink or two. Some of the people started to leave, and so we got a few tables to push together so we could sit down. My boyfriend had arrived, and he sat on one side of me and Jamie sat on the other side.

Hamilton was not there at first, and after I sat down I saw him for the first time. Hamilton sat next to Jamie, and Singleton was sitting across from Hamilton. After we got seated, Hamilton bought a round of drinks for everyone.

I spent most of my time talking to my boyfriend and the people across from us. Occasionally, I said something to Jamie, but she spent most of her time talking to Hamilton and Singleton. We may have been seated about an hour when Jamie moved closer to me. At first I did not think anything of it, but a short time later she moved closer again. Before I could say anything to her, Jamie said she needed more room and glanced at Hamilton. I could see that he was getting close to Jamie, so I moved over to give her more room.

A few minutes later, Jamie asked me when I was leaving. I had just gotten another drink, and I told her I would give her a ride home when I finished it. I do not know what Jamie and Hamilton said to each other, but about ten minutes later, Jamie told me that she was leaving and Hamilton was driving her home. I was having a good time, so I was pleased that I did not have to leave.

About thirty minutes after they left, Jamie called me on my cell phone. I had had about four or five drinks by then, and the bar was noisy. Jamie made some comment to me about Hamilton kissing her good night. I told her that Hamilton was not the worst guy she had kissed, and she commented that he was the oldest. Our conversation was short, but I did not feel that Jamie was upset.

I did not talk to Jamie until I picked her up for work on Monday. I told Jamie that she would be hired permanently for sure if she started dating Hamilton. Jamie told me that she had no intention of going out with Hamilton and that they both had been drinking when they kissed. She did not seem upset about the incident, but I could tell that she did not want to be teased about it.

Jamie and I saw Hamilton in his office with Singleton when we walked into the warehouse. Jamie went directly to her work station, and I went to mine. I cannot see the other line from where I work, so I do not know what happened that day. Jamie did not say anything about either Hamilton or Singleton on our way home that evening.

Hamilton generally walked through the warehouse several times a day. At times, he would stop and talk to someone. Because Singleton was responsible for the two packaging lines, he could not watch us all the time. I saw him in Hamilton's office many times, and he made calls to other parts of the plant to check on production and shipping.

We were entitled to two fifteen-minute breaks during the day and a thirty-minute lunch break. We could not take the breaks at the same time because we had to keep the line moving. We did not have to punch a time clock when we took a break. Sometimes I would see Jamie when I had a break. I know Jamie did not always get back to her work station on time. A few times she would stay with me if I went into the break room when she already was there. I also saw Jamie talking to other workers at times as she was returning to her job. Everyone took a few extra minutes some days, and Jamie was no different than anyone else.

I was not aware that Jamie was having any problems with Singleton until later in the week. Jamie complained that Singleton was watching her all the time and criticizing her work. I had not had any problems with Singleton, and I encouraged Jamie to hang in there and do her best.

If someone got a written reprimand, he had to meet with Hamilton and Singleton. The employee had to sign the reprimand, and there is a place for the employee to write in any comments. I believe the reprimand then is put in the employee's file. The following Monday, I heard through the gossip mill that Jamie had received a write-up and was seen in Hamilton's office. After work, Jamie told me that she had received the reprimand and had met with Singleton and Hamilton. After Singleton left, Jamie said that Hamilton asked her out and reminded her that he had the final decision on her future with the company.

One day, Jamie was wearing a T-shirt that said, "If you can read this, you're staring." I told her that the shirt would get her some attention, and she laughed. I was not aware that Singleton had complained about the rolled up T-shirt. If I had heard about that, I may have said something to Jamie about her latest T-shirt. When Jamie met me after work, the T-shirt was inside out. Jamie told me that Singleton had made her reverse the shirt on one of her breaks.

On June 4, YR-2, Jamie called me as I was getting ready to leave my apartment. She told me that she had overslept and that she would drive herself to work. I do not know what time she got to work, but later I saw Jamie, and she told me that she had received another reprimand from Singleton.

Jamie also complained about her meeting with Hamilton. Apparently, Hamilton had made some comment about sleeping with her boyfriend and brushed against her when she was leaning over the desk to sign the write-up. Jamie also said that Hamilton had asked her out again but that she would not go out with him even if it meant losing her job.

On June 10, YR-2, I dropped a box on my foot and had to leave the plant to have it x-rayed. Before I left, I told Jamie that she would have to find a ride home.

A few days before my accident, Jamie had another run-in with Singleton. It was a hot day, and I saw Jamie as she was leaving the break room after lunch. Her hair was wet and so was her T-shirt. I did not say anything to her, but I was not surprised when she later told me that Singleton had complained about her wet T-shirt. Jamie also laughed and said that if Hamilton had walked past her, the wet T-shirt would have guaranteed her a permanent job.

I was off work until Monday, June 22, YR-2. I had talked to Jamie several times while I was off, but she did not say anything about either Singleton or Hamilton. However, when she called me Sunday to confirm that I would give her a ride to work, she asked if we could leave early because she did not want to be late. I told her that I had to go to the Human Resources Department before I could start working and that leaving early was a good idea. We got to the plant about twenty minutes early, and Jamie went directly to the warehouse. I know that she started work before 8:00 a.m.

Later that day, I heard that Jamie had been fired. I know some other probationary workers had not been hired full time, but this was the first time I saw someone fired before the end of the sixty-day period.

I called Jamie later that day when I got home. Jamie said that she had told Hamilton she was fired because she had not gone out with him. Jamie said Hamilton made some comment about missing out on two good opportunities.

I did once go to HR a few months before Jamie was hired and told Michelle Johnson that I was having a problem with Hamilton sexually harassing me, but it was really just BS. I thought his behavior was a little weird, but nothing out of the ordinary when you're working around a bunch of guys. I only complained because I wanted to be on record in case something happened later that I really didn't like.

I do have some entries in my diary at home where I record stuff about work. A few times I recall putting in some stuff about Jamie's problems at work, but mostly it's personal stuff of my own. Yes, I think sometimes I wrote down stuff about the way Hamilton acted at work. I will check the diary and get you copies of any pages that have to do with Jamie or Hamilton. I think I may also have some emails from Jamie about Hamilton, and I'll check for those too.

Lisa Roberts

[Assume that the day before the deposition is due to be taken in this training course, Roberts came to plaintiff's counsel's office to be prepared and brought with her the document included in this file as Exhibit R-1 (available only to plaintiff), which has not heretofore been produced in discovery. She says she did not find any diary entries of the kind she thought she recalled. Further assume that the Notice of Deposition included a standard duces tecum clause requesting the witness to bring "any and all documents relating to or concerning:

1. *Jamie Taylor's employment at Pinnacle Packaging*
2. *Hamilton's behavior toward female employees."*

You should also assume that the subpoenas that require the attendance of the other witnesses in the case file contain the same duces tecum clause.]

Exhibit R-1

Taylor's Email to Roberts

From: jtaylor@aol.nita

To: lisarob@mindspring.nita

Re: work idea

Date: May 26, YR-2

You know how I told you Hamilton has put a few moves on me at work, after that first time at the bar my first week? It's not too bad—we're used to that sort of thing, aren't we, from guys at work—but I'm not going to let it go if it gets worse. Plus, they're starting to hassle me now about working slow and taking long breaks. Do you think I have to start reporting him every time he gets physical?

Statement of Jerry Black

My name is Jerry Black, and I have worked at Pinnacle Packaging Products since June YR-6. Sometime in May YR-2, Jamie Taylor was hired by the company and assigned to my packaging line. John Hamilton is the warehouse manager, and Chuck Singleton is the foreman of my line and another line located nearby.

I am not good at remembering dates, but shortly after Jamie started we went out for drinks at Kool's Korner to celebrate Singleton's birthday. We were all standing around because the bar was crowded and there was no place for all of us to sit. I remember talking to Jamie briefly that evening, but I only stayed for one drink. I do not remember whether Hamilton got there before I left, but some of the employees were pushing tables together so they could sit down. I left before people got seated. On Monday, I did not hear any gossip about what may have happened after I left.

I have seen a number of people come and go from my packaging line. It can be hard work because you have to keep busy and lift some heavy boxes. Jamie is an average-sized woman and had problems lifting some heavy boxes. She appeared to work hard and catch on to the program. I was not watching her all the time, and we were not partners. However, she was doing a good job, especially for a new employee.

Jamie is very friendly and talked to anyone who was in the area. She also was attractive and somewhat of a tease. The warehouse is not air conditioned and can get hot in the summer. One day, Jamie rolled up the sleeves on her T-shirt and tied the bottom of her T-shirt showing off some of her belly. Of course, the guys on the line approved of her appearance and some comments were made. Jamie responded to some of the comments and seemed to enjoy the attention. A short time later, Singleton came to the line and told Jamie to untie the knot in her T-shirt. Jamie did what she was told, and some of the guys made a few comments to Singleton about spoiling the fun.

About one week later, Jamie wore a T-shirt that said "If you can read this, you're staring." Several comments were made by some of the guys. I made a comment about being a slow reader, and Janet Long said something about me being illiterate. Hamilton saw the T-shirt when he walked by. I could not hear what he and Jamie said, but they were laughing. Jamie seemed to enjoy the banter until Singleton showed up and complained about the T-shirt. He told her to turn the shirt inside out on her next break. Jamie said, "You want me to turn it inside out right here—I don't mind." All the guys started to cheer, but Singleton didn't seem amused.

One or two weeks later, Singleton was upset with Jamie after she returned from lunch. It was another hot day in the warehouse, and Jamie had put her head under the faucet or something to cool off. Her hair and T-shirt were wet when she returned to the work area. Of course, some of the other guys and I noticed and made some comments. I believe I suggested a company wet T-shirt contest. Jamie and Janet made some comments back to us, and I thought the incident was over. However, Singleton walked up and was noticeably upset by Jamie's appearance.

For some reason, Singleton seemed to have it in for Jamie almost from the start. We are entitled to a fifteen-minute break in the morning, another fifteen-minute break in the afternoon, and thirty minutes for lunch. We do not have to punch a time clock for our breaks, and sometimes someone gets back a little late. Singleton seemed to be watching Jamie and noticed when she was not back to work on time or stopped to talk to someone while she was walking back to the line.

Jamie never said anything to me about Hamilton. Whenever Hamilton walked through the warehouse, Jamie made a point to talk to him. Their conversations were not long, and most of the time I could not hear what they were saying. I considered Jamie a flirt, and she acted that way with Hamilton.

I am aware that Jamie received some write-ups from Singleton and that she was called into Hamilton's office several times because of it. She never told me any details, but she did say that Singleton was picking on her. I was surprised when Jamie was fired before her probationary period ended. I know of some people who were not hired full time after sixty days, but I am not aware of anyone who was not allowed to complete the probationary period. I thought that Jamie was trying hard and doing the best that she could. Some probationary employees who did not work as hard as Jamie were allowed to complete the sixty-day period before they were fired.

Exhibits Available to Both Plaintiff and Defendant

Exhibit 1

DISCIPLINARY ACTION

Date: 5/25/YR-2

Employee: Jamie Taylor

Evaluation: Employee is working slowly and not meeting quotas

Employee is spending too much time away from work station

C Singleton
Foreman

John Hamilton
Manager

Employee Comments:

Jamie Taylor
Employee

Exhibit 2

DISCIPLINARY ACTION

Date: 6/4/YR-2

Employee: Jamie Taylor

Evaluation: Employee was 10 minutes late today

Employee has dressed inappropriately on 2 different dates

Employee is slow worker

C Singleton — Foreman

John Hamilton — Manager

Employee Comments:

Jamie Taylor — Employee

Exhibit 3

DISCIPLINARY ACTION

Date: 6/19/YR-2

Employee: Jamie Taylor

Evaluation: Employee was 20 minutes late today

Not meeting quotas

Employee is spending too much time away from work station

C Singleton — Foreman

John Hamilton — Manager

Employee Comments:

Jamie Taylor — Employee

Exhibit 4

STATE OF NITA

DARROW CIRCUIT COURT

IN RE: THE MARRIAGE OF NANCY HAMILTON and	: :	CAUSE NO. YR-2 CIVIL 812
	: :	
JOHN HAMILTON Defendant	: :	

TEMPORARY RESTRAINING ORDER

This matter has come before the court on the Petition for Restraining Order filed by Nancy Hamilton on March 3, YR-2. The court has reviewed the affidavit supporting the Petition and now GRANTS the relief requested.

IT IS NOW ORDERED that John Hamilton vacate the premises known as 1624 Oak Street, Nita City, and remain away from that residence until further order of court.

IT IS FURTHER ORDERED that John Hamilton refrain from contacting Nancy Hamilton in any fashion until further order of court.

IT IS FURTHER ORDERED that John Hamilton not enter the Nita City Food Mart, the place of employment of Nancy Hamilton, until further order of court.

IT IS FURTHER ORDERED that John Hamilton not follow, stalk, or in any manner threaten or harass Nancy Hamilton until further order of court.

ENTERED this 3rd day of March, YR-2

Katherine Parks

Judge, Darrow County Circuit Court

Exhibit 5

Excerpt from Pinnacle Packaging Policies Manual

Pinnacle Packaging Products Prohibited Harassment Policy

Prohibited Harassment

Pinnacle Packaging Products is committed to providing a work environment free of harassment. Pinnacle maintains a strict policy prohibiting sexual harassment and harassment because of race, color, sex, sexual orientation, gender identity or expression, religion, national origin, age, disability, or any other basis protected by applicable law. All such harassment is prohibited. Pinnacle's anti-harassment policy applies to all persons involved in the operations of the company, including applicants, and prohibits harassment by any employee of Pinnacle Packaging Products, including managers and coworkers.

Sexual Harassment Defined

Federal law defines sexual harassment as unwanted sexual advances, requests for sexual favors, or visual, verbal, or physical conduct of a sexual nature when:

- submission to such conduct is made a term or condition of employment; or
- submission to or rejection of such conduct is used as a basis for employment decisions affecting the individual; or
- such conduct has the purpose or effect of unreasonably interfering with an employee's work performance or creating an intimidating, hostile, or offensive working environment.

State and local law definitions of sexual harassment include various forms of offensive behavior. The following is a partial list:

- Unwanted sexual advances.
- Offering employment benefits in exchange for sexual favors.
- Making or threatening reprisals after a negative response to sexual advances.
- Visual conduct: leering, making sexual gestures, displaying of sexually suggestive objects or pictures, cartoons, or posters.
- Verbal conduct: making or using derogatory comments, epithets, slurs, sexually explicit jokes, comments about an employee's body or dress.

- Verbal sexual advances or propositions.
- Verbal abuse of a sexual nature, graphic verbal commentary about an individual's body, sexually degrading words to describe an individual, suggestive or obscene letters, notes, or invitations.
- Physical conduct: touching, assault, impeding, or blocking movements.
- Retaliation for making harassment reports or threatening to report harassment.

Pinnacle's policy also protects employees from harassment by vendors or clients. If harassment occurs on the job by someone not employed by the Company, the procedures in this policy should be followed as if the harasser were an employee of the Company.

It is unlawful for males to sexually harass females or other males, and for females to sexually harass males or other females.

Other Types of Harassment

Prohibited harassment on the basis of race, color, sex, sexual orientation, gender identity or expression, religion, national origin, age, disability, or any other basis protected by applicable law, includes behavior similar to sexual harassment such as:

- Verbal conduct such as threats, epithets, derogatory comments, or slurs;
- Visual conduct such as derogatory posters, photography, cartoons, drawings, or gestures;
- Physical conduct such as assault, unwanted touching, or blocking normal movement;
- Retaliation for making harassment reports or threatening to report harassment.

Pinnacle's Complaint Procedure

Pinnacle's reporting procedure provides for a prompt, thorough, and objective investigation of any claim of harassment or discrimination. If the Company determines that prohibited activity has occurred, it will take appropriate remedial action. The discipline will be commensurate with the severity of the offense. Appropriate action will also be taken to deter any future prohibited activity. All reported incidents of harassment or discrimination will be investigated. Designated representatives of the Company will promptly undertake an effective, thorough, and objective investigation of the allegations. When the investigation is completed, a determination regarding the allegations will be made and communicated to the person who filed the report as soon as practical.

An individual subjected to what he or she believes is sexual, racial, or other improper harassment should immediately tell the harasser to stop the unwanted behavior and/or immediately report that behavior, preferably in writing, to the human resources director. If any further incident(s) of harassment occur, the incident(s) must be immediately reported.

If an employee becomes aware of harassing conduct engaged in or directed toward a Pinnacle Packaging Products employee, the employee should immediately report that information, preferably in writing, to the human resources director.

Pinnacle strictly prohibits retaliation against any person by another employee or by the Company for using this complaint procedure, reporting harassment, or for filing, testifying, assisting, or participating in any manner in any investigation, proceeding, or hearing conducted by a governmental enforcement agency. Prohibited retaliation includes, but is not limited to, termination, demotion, suspension, failure to hire or consider for hire, failure to give equal consideration in making employment decisions, failure to make employment recommendations impartially, adversely affecting working conditions, or otherwise denying any employment benefit.

Any person who is found to have engaged in unlawful harassment is subject to disciplinary action up to and including discharge from employment. A person who engages in harassment may be held personally liable for monetary damages.

Pinnacle does not consider conduct in violation of this policy to be within the course and scope of employment or the direct consequence of the discharge of one's duties. Accordingly, to the extent permitted by law, the Company reserves the right not to provide a defense or pay damages assessed against an employee for conduct in violation of this policy.

Exhibit 6

MEMO TO: **File**

FROM: **Michelle Johnson**

RE: **Complaint of Sexual Harassment by Jamie Taylor**

DATE: **August 6, YR-2**

Former employee Jamie Taylor (terminated June 22, YR-2) filed a complaint with the EEOC alleging that employee John Hamilton, her supervisor in the packing room, had sexually harassed her and that her termination was in retribution for her refusal to accede to his demands for dating, sex, or both.

I investigated this matter by collecting information from:

John Hamilton—warehouse manager

Chuck Singleton—warehouse foreman

Lisa Roberts—co-worker of Taylor's on packing line

Jerry Black—co-worker of Taylor's on packing line

Hamilton denied that he had ever harassed Taylor or asked her out on a date, except as a joke and during some good-natured banter.

Singleton corroborated Hamilton's recollection in that he (Singleton) had never observed any inappropriate behavior or touching by Hamilton towards Taylor. Singleton says that if anything it was the reverse: Taylor seemed to be flirting with Hamilton and trying to get him interested.

Lisa Roberts declined to discuss the matter. She said that she was too good a friend of Taylor's and did not want to get either Taylor or Hamilton in trouble—"let sleeping dogs lies" were her words.

Jerry Black said that in his opinion the kind of flirting that always went on in the packing room was what everyone was used to, and Hamilton's participation in it seemed to him to be just a question of "the boss trying to fit in"—nothing more. He also said that he thought there was something odd about Taylor being fired so early in her employment here, because to his view she did not perform any worse than others in tardiness, length of breaks, inappropriate comments, or dress, etc.

Given Black's comment, I re-interviewed Hamilton and Singleton on the reasons for their decision to terminate Taylor, and they were adamant and convincing in their position that she was terminated for repeated tardiness and other incidents for which she had received disciplinary write-ups.

Conclusion: Taylor's complaints are unfounded and unsubstantiated. File closed.

Exhibit 7

MEMO TO: File

FROM: Michelle Johnson

RE: Complaint of Sexual Harassment by Lisa Roberts

DATE: February 27, YR-2

Current employee Roberts has filed an oral complaint with this office alleging that her supervisor, John Hamilton, told her that she could get a promotion if she "played ball with him," which she alleges constituted a sexual overture. She further alleges that when he said this to her, during a work-progress review session with him in his office, he put his hand on her knee and rubbed it. She further alleges that this incident followed other times when she claims Hamilton flirted with her when passing her station on the packing line—but she gave no specifics in my interview with her, nor did she add any detail beyond the behavior she initially complained about.

I have interviewed Hamilton about this. He says that Roberts misunderstood him. He did tell her that she would be eligible for a promotion if she, in his words, "tried hard to learn the ropes of mid-level management" from him and Chuck Singleton (her immediate supervisor). As to inappropriate touching, Hamilton said that while he was talking with Roberts during the review session, he tripped over a leg of his office table and fell towards her, and in steadying himself he may have accidentally touched her leg or knee.

Conclusion: I find Hamilton's recollection to be more credible than Roberts's. Accordingly, the complaint is ruled unfounded. As a precaution against future incidents, Hamilton will be required to attend a sensitivity training session.

Exhibit 8

Equal Employment Opportunity Commission

Pinnacle Packaging Products Inc.
1 Industrial Way
Nita City, Nita

Person Filing Charge	Jamie Taylor
This Person	[X] Claims to be aggrieved [ ] Is filling on behalf of another
Date of Alleged Violation	5/15/YR-2
Place of Alleged Violation	Nita City, Nita
Charge Number	YR-2-03782

Notice of Charge of Discrimination

(See EEOC "Rules and Regulations" before completing this Form)

You are hereby notified that a charge of employment discrimination has been filed against your organization under:

[X] Title VII of the Civil Rights Act of 1964

[ ] The Age Discrimination in Employment Act of 1967

[ ] The Americans with Disabilities Act

[ ] The Equal Pay Act (28 U.S.C., Sect. 204(d) *Investigation will be conducted concurrently with our investigation of this charge.*

The boxes checked below apply to your organization:

[ ] No action is required on your part at this time.

[X] Please submit by 8/17/YR-2 a statement of your position with respect to the allegation(s) contained in this charge, with copies of any supporting documentation. This material will be made a part of the file and will be considered at the time that we investigate this charge. Your prompt response to this request will make it easier to conduct and conclude our investigation of this charge.

[ ] Please respond fully by ______ to the attached request for information which pertains to the allegations contained in this charge. Such information will be made a part of the file and will be considered by the Commission during the course of its investigation of the charge.

For further inquiry on this matter, please use the charge number shown above. Your position statement, your response to your request for information, or any inquiry you may have should be directed to:

Terry Mattoon
Commission Representative

555-4444
Telephone Number

[ ] Enclosure:

Basis of Discrimination: [ ] Race [ ] Color [X] Sex [ ] Religion [ ] Nat. Origin [ ] Age [ ] Disability [ ] Retaliation [ ] Other

Circumstances of Alleged Violation	Claimant claims she was sexually harassed and propositioned by her supervisor, John Hamilton, and that her termination was in retaliation for her refusal of his sexual advances.

Date: 7/17/YR-2 Name/Title of Authorized EEOC Official: Terry Mattoon Signature: Terry Mattoon

Exhibit 9

Pinnacle Packaging Products, Inc.

One Industrial Way

Nita City, Nita 99991

August 11, YR-2

Ms. Terry Mattoon

Equal Employment Opportunity Commission

22 Constitution Plaza

Nita City, Nita

Dear Ms. Mattoon:

I am writing on behalf of Pinnacle Packaging Products Inc., in response to your correspondence of July 17, YR-2, in which you provided to us a Notice of Charge of Discrimination by Ms. Jamie Taylor.

Pinnacle Packaging categorically denies that Ms. Taylor was sexually harassed by any employee of Pinnacle, or that her termination was in retaliation for any action by Ms. Taylor, as she claims. Ms. Taylor was terminated via proper procedures under Pinnacle's hiring and employment policies; the termination was made during her initial probationary period, during which she (a) showed herself unsuited to the position for which she was hired, and (b) acted in disregard of Pinnacle's work rules and regulations, despite fair and repeated warnings.

If you have any further questions concerning this unfounded allegation, please feel free to contact me.

Sincerely,

Michele Johnson

Exhibit 10

Equal Employment Opportunity Commission
Notice of Right to Sue
(Issued on request)

To: Ms. Jamie Taylor
1234 Main Street
Nita City, Nita

☐ On behalf of a person aggrieved whose identity is confidential (29 C.F.R. 1601.7(a))

From: Equal Employment Opportunity Commission
22 Constitution Plaza
Nita City, Nita

Charge Number: YR-2-03782 | EEOC Representative: Terry Mattoon | Telephone Number: 555-4444

(See additional information attached to this form)

TO THE PERSON AGGRIEVED: This is your NOTICE OF RIGHT TO SUE. It is issued at your request. If you intend to use the respondent(s) named in your charge, YOU MUST DO SO WITHIN NINETY (90) DAYS OF YOUR RECEIPT OF THIS NOTICE: OTHERWISE YOUR RIGHT TO SUE IS LOST.

☒ More than 180 days have expired since the filing of this charge

☐ Less than 180 days have expired since the filing of this charge, but I have determined that the Commission will be unable to complete the process with 180 days from the filing of the charge.

☒ With the issuance of this NOTICE OF RIGHT TO SUE, the Commission is terminating its process with respect to this charge.

☐ It has been determined that the Commission will continue to investigate your charge.

☐ ADEA: While Title VII and the ADA require EEOC to issue this Notice of Right to Sue before you can bring a lawsuit you may sue under the Age Discrimination in Employment ct (ADEA) any time 60 days after your charge was filed until 90 days after you received notice that EEOC has completed action on your charge.

☐ Because EEOC is closing your case, your lawsuit under the ADEA must be brought within 90 days of your receipt of this notice. Otherwise, your right to sue is lost.

☐ EEOC is continuing its investigation. You will be notified when we have completed action and, if your notice will include notice of right to sue under the ADEA.

☐ EPA: While Title VII and the ADA require EEOC to issue this Notice of Right to Sue before you can bring a lawsuit you already have the right to sue under the Equal Pay Act (EPA) (You are not required to complain to any enforcement agency before bringing an EPA suit in court) EPA suits must be brought within 2 years (3 years for willful violations) of the alleged EPA underpayment.

I certify that this notice was mailed on the date set out below.

1/19/YR-1
Date mailed

On behalf of the Commission

Terry Mattoon

Enclosures:
Information Sheet
Copy of Charge

CC: Respondents

Exhibit 11

Diagram of Pinnacle Warehouse

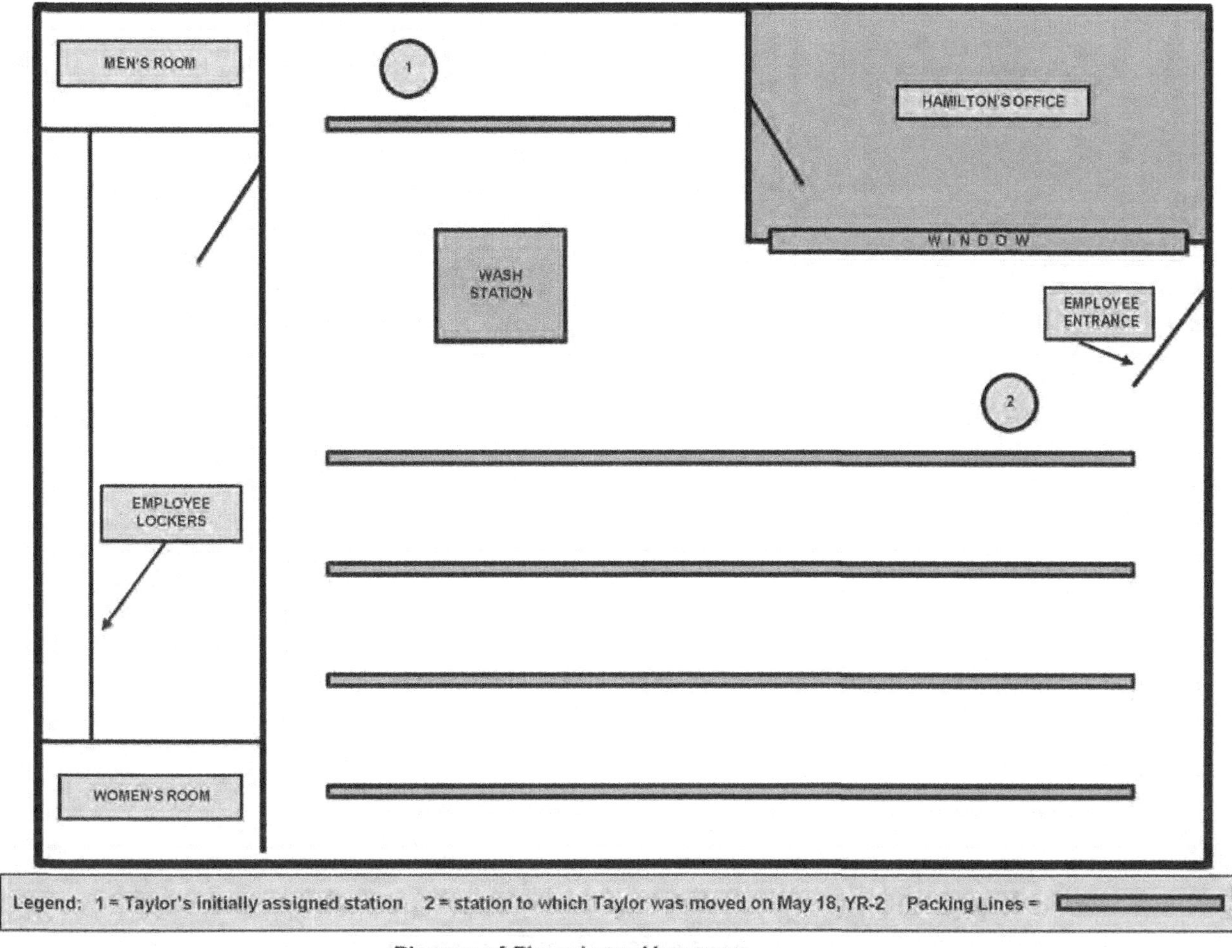

Diagram of Pinnacle packing room

Preliminary Jury Instructions

Duty of Jurors

You have been selected as jurors and have taken an oath to well and truly try this case.

During the trial, there will be times when you will be allowed to separate, such as recesses and lunch periods. When you are outside the courtroom, you must not talk about this case among yourselves or with anyone else.

During the trial, do not talk to any of the parties, their lawyers, or any of the witnesses. If anyone makes any attempt to talk to you concerning this case, you should report the fact to the court immediately.

You should keep an open mind. You should not form or express an opinion or reach any conclusion in this case until you have heard all of the evidence, the arguments of counsel, and the final instructions as to the law.

Issues for Trial

The plaintiff, Jamie Taylor, was hired by the defendant, Pinnacle Packaging Products, as a probationary employee for a sixty-day period. The plaintiff was fired before the end of the probationary period. The plaintiff contends that she was fired because she refused to date the warehouse manager, John Hamilton, who made the ultimate decision to terminate her employment.

The defendant denies that Hamilton made advances toward the plaintiff and contends that the plaintiff was fired for her poor job performance. The defendant also contends that it has a company policy prohibiting sexual harassment in any form and that the plaintiff failed to follow the company policy and report any harassment.

Preponderance of the Evidence

When I say that a party has the burden to prove an issue by a preponderance of the evidence, I mean by the greater weight of the evidence. A greater number of witnesses testifying to a fact on one side, or a greater quantity of evidence introduced on one side, is not necessarily of the greater weight. The evidence given upon any fact that convinces you oat strongly of its truthfulness is of the greater weight.

Credibility of Witnesses

You are the sole judges of the credibility of "believability" of each witness and the weight to be given to his testimony. In weighing the testimony of a witness, you should consider his relationship to the plaintiff or to the defendant; his interest, if any, in the outcome of the case; his manner of testifying; his opportunity to observe or acquire knowledge concerning the facts about which he testified; his candor, fairness, and intelligence; and the extent to which he had been supported or contradicted by other credible evidence. You may, in short, accept or reject the testimony of any witness in whole or in part.

Concluding Instruction

After I complete these preliminary instructions, the plaintiff and the defendant will have the opportunity to address you in an opening statement. Following the opening statements, first the plaintiff will present evidence and then the defendant will present evidence. After all the evidence has been presented, the parties again will have the opportunity to address you with their final arguments. At the conclusion of this case, I will give you the final instructions to guide your deliberations and assist you in reaching your verdict.

Final Jury Instructions

Burden of Proof

When I say a particular party must prove something by "a preponderance of the evidence," or when I use the expression "if you find," or "if you decide," this is what I mean: When you have considered all the evidence in the case, you must be persuaded that it is more probably true than not true.

Cautionary Instruction on Reasonableness of Defendant's Action

In deciding the plaintiff's claim, you should not concern yourself with whether the defendant's actions were wise, reasonable, or fair. Rather, your concern is only whether the plaintiff has proved that the defendant was terminated her because of sex.

Title VII

The plaintiff claims that she was discharged because she failed to submit to the sexual advances of her supervisor, John Hamilton. To succeed on this claim, the plaintiff must prove the following elements by a preponderance of the evidence:

1. She is a member of a protected class, a female;
2. Her job performance met the defendant's legitimate expectations;
3. She suffered an adverse employment action, a discharge; and
4. Another similarly situated individual who was not in the protected class was treated more favorably.

If you find that the plaintiff has proved each of these items by a preponderance of the evidence, then you must find for the plaintiff. However, if the plaintiff has not met her burden of proof, then you must find for the defendant.

If you find that the plaintiff's discharge was motivated by both (1) her refusal to accept sexual advances from a management employee of the defendant and (2) the plaintiff's poor job performance, then the plaintiff is entitled to prevail on her claim unless the defendant proves by a preponderance of the evidence that it would have discharged the plaintiff regardless of whether the alleged improper sexual advances did or did not occur.

Affirmative Defense

The employer has an affirmative defense to a Title VII claim if it had a policy against any form of sexual harassment and/or discrimination. That policy must be made known to the employees and must include a procedure for filing any complaints of discrimination.

If you find that the defendant had a policy against any form of sexual harassment and/or discrimination and that the plaintiff unreasonably failed to follow the company procedures, then your verdict should be for the defendant.

The defendant has the burden of proof on its affirmative defense.

Damages: General

If you find that the plaintiff has proved her claim against the defendant, then you must determine what amount of damages, if any, the plaintiff is entitled to recover. The plaintiff must prove her damages by a preponderance of the evidence.

If you find that the plaintiff has failed to prove any of her claims, then you will not consider the question of damages.

Compensatory Damages

You may award compensatory damages only for injuries that the plaintiff has proved by a preponderance of the evidence were caused by the defendant's wrongful conduct.

Your award must be based on evidence and not speculation or guesswork. This does not mean, however, that compensatory damages are restricted to the actual loss of money; they include both the physical and mental aspects of injury, even if they are not easy to measure.

In calculating damages, you should not consider the issue of lost wages and benefits. The court will calculate and determine any damages for past or future lost wages and benefits. You should consider the following for compensatory damages, and no others:

The mental and emotional pain and suffering that the plaintiff has experienced. No evidence of the dollar value of mental and emotional pain and suffering has been or needs to be introduced. There is no exact standard for setting the damages to be awarded on account of pain and suffering. You are to determine an amount that will fairly compensate the plaintiff for the injury she has sustained.

Proximate Cause

Proximate cause is that cause that produces the injury complained of and without which the injury would not have occurred.

Deliberations

When you retire to deliberate, select one of your number as the foreperson. After you have reached unanimous agreement on your verdict, the foreperson must date and sign the verdict form.

Made in the USA
Monee, IL
04 January 2023